*The
Connell Short Guide
to*

The Gothic

by Catherine Redford

Contents

What is the Gothic?	3
Where did the Gothic originate?	4
Eighteenth-century and Romantic Gothic	7
Fin de Siècle Gothic	16
Twentieth-century British Gothic	26
Southern Gothic	33

NOTES

Five Facts about The Gothic	*24*
The Gothic: A short chronology	*42*
Further reading	*44*

What is the Gothic?

When we think of the Gothic, a wide variety of dark and frightening images spring to mind. From stormy nights and gloomy forests to haunted houses and decaying castles, ghosts and demons to murderers and villains, skeletons and hidden chambers to foreign lands and the distant past, the list goes on. But while the presence of these things seems to indicate that we are reading a Gothic text, there's certainly no such thing as a "check-list" of elements that a text must contain in order to be classed as Gothic.

Indeed, some texts are – somewhat confusingly – Gothic without containing any of the elements listed above. Some Gothic novels are, indeed, set in dark, mysterious locations in Europe, but others set the scene amongst the white picket fences, perfect housewives, and manicured lawns of the American suburbs. As well as medieval castles and ruined abbeys, the reader of Gothic fiction will also find scientific laboratories and even ordinary, modern houses; far from always being set in the past, plenty of Gothic texts tell stories of the present day. Gothic literature is undoubtedly filled with all sorts of ghosts, monsters, demons, and vampires, but many Gothic texts locate the monstrous not within spectres and supernatural creatures but within humans – people just like you or me.

The Gothic can be fantastic or familiar, suggestive or explicit, filled with horror or prompting terror: there's no set formula. What the group of texts defined as "Gothic" do all have in common, however, is an ability to invoke fear. The genre emerged in the 18th century and has continued to adapt and develop ever since, often reacting to the anxieties and concerns of the period in which it is written. This book will consider a series of key moments in the history of the Gothic, exploring how our understanding of it shifts in response to changes in society, culture, and politics. As well as examining how the Gothic has altered across time, this guide will also investigate the threads running through the genre's history that unite a collection of seemingly quite different texts under the same rubric.

Where did the Gothic originate?

The word "Gothic" originally referred to the barbarian tribes of northern Europe who were believed to have brought down the Roman Empire when they invaded central and southern Europe in the fifth century. Because Roman society was closely associated with order and reason, the Visigoths were consequently seen as savage, brutal, and irrational. The refinement of Rome had been replicated in the trend for the Neoclassical in the early 18th century, a fashion that saw contemporary literature, art, and architecture draw inspiration from the classical culture of Ancient Greece and Rome.

In the middle of the 18th century, however, the idea of the "Gothic" entered English culture; in many ways a reaction against Neoclassicism, this understanding of the Gothic lost its specific geographical significance and came simply to encapsulate anything associated with the Dark Ages. As David Punter has noted:

> Where the classical was well-ordered, the Gothic was chaotic; where simple and pure, Gothic was ornate and convoluted; where the classics offered a set of cultural models to be followed, Gothic represented excess and exaggeration, the product of the wild and uncivilised.

These qualities of the Gothic proved very appealing, and people wanted to rediscover this exciting "lost" period of history. This interest prompted a Gothic revival in architecture, and in the 1740s wealthy landowners began designing homes that looked like medieval castles and building fake Gothic ruins in their grounds. Horace Walpole, who would go on to write the first Gothic novel, *The Castle of Otranto*, started to construct his own Gothic Revival castle, "Strawberry Hill House", in Twickenham in the mid-18th century. Likewise, William Beckford, who wrote the Gothic novel *Vathek*, built a neo-Gothic abbey that collapsed under the weight of its own huge tower in 1825.

In literature, so-called "Graveyard Poetry" became popular, featuring titles such as *Night-Thoughts* (Edward Young, 1742), *The Grave* (Robert Blair, 1743), and "Ode to Fear" (William Collins, 1746). The Graveyard Poets were primarily interested in writing reflective, melancholy meditations on death and mortality, and their work abounds with graves, skulls, and worms.

This period also saw the growing popularity of folk poetry, with Thomas Percy's *Reliques of Ancient English Poetry* (1765) collecting together works written in the traditional ballad form. As narrative songs passed down orally from generation to generation, these ballads appealed due to their lack of pretension and their links with the past; they were also seen as less artificial than the early 18th-century Neoclassicist poetry written by "Augustans" such as Alexander Pope.

With these foundations laid, it wasn't long until the first Gothic novel appeared. Published on Christmas Eve, 1764, Horace Walpole's *The Castle of Otranto* tells the story of Manfred, the Prince of Otranto, and his quest to ensure that his family line is not lost. In his Preface to the first edition of the novel, Walpole claimed that he had found the work, which had supposedly been printed in 1529, "in the library of an ancient Catholic family in the north of England"; it was only in the Preface to the second edition that he admitted he was the author rather than just the translator of the text.

The Castle of Otranto features many tropes that

have come to be viewed as markers of the Gothic, including the figure of the pursued heroine, secret passageways, and mysterious noises, as well as the castle itself. Walpole's supernatural, however, can come across as excessive – even ludicrous – to the modern reader. Manfred's son, Conrad, for example, is killed by a giant helmet that crushes him to death, and the castle's portraits sigh and move.

18th-Century and Romantic Gothic

The Castle of Otranto is set in medieval Italy, and this distant historical and geographical positioning allowed Walpole to draw on the dark barbarism associated with the Catholic past in his exploration of the Gothic. Since the Reformation in the 16th century, England had been a Protestant country, and Catholicism was perceived as a foreign religion, associated with rebellion and danger. A similar distancing technique is also used by William Beckford, who in his novel *Vathek* combined Walpole's excess with the rich exoticism of the Oriental to produce a fantastical tale of terror. A wealthy and eccentric individual, as a youth Beckford loved to read a collection of Middle Eastern and Indian stories that had been translated into English in 1706 as *The Arabian Nights' Entertainment*. When he wrote *Vathek* in French in

1782, he drew on this 18th-century interest in the Orient, creating a tale filled with magnificent palaces, rich perfumes, and eastern magic.* The way in which Beckford, as a westerner, imagines – and thus "invents" – the life and customs of the East from an outsider's perspective is known as "Orientalism".

Beckford's novel is Gothic in its use of the supernatural: the text is filled with ghosts, ghouls, and spirits. Vathek – a rich and powerful ruler – enters a Satanic bargain with a demon named the "Giaour" in order to gain supernatural powers, but the text ends with him entering hell and facing torturous punishment for failing to remain "humble and ignorant". Beckford's depiction of hell is both lavish and terrifying; as Vathek enters this realm along a pavement strewn with gold dust he smells exotic incense, sees tables piled high with food and wine, and is greeted by a throng of spirits who "danced lasciviously". He becomes "frozen with terror", however, when he sees others who have been damned to this place, some of whom shriek with agony while others grind their teeth and foam at the mouth like the "wildest maniac".

Despite its ability to instil terror in the reader, *Vathek* is also comic in its excess and perversity. When Vathek's mother, Carathis, summons a collection of ghouls from their tombs in a cemetery

---

* *Vathek* was translated into English by Samuel Henry in 1786, although this edition was read, corrected, and annotated by Beckford himself.

Mary Shelley (1797 – 1851), author of Frankenstein

to feed on corpses and offer advice from beyond the grave, the reader expects to be frightened by the ensuing episode. Carathis, however, proceeds to converse with these supernatural beings in an entirely civilised fashion, with the narrator explaining how "The Princess received her visitants with distinguished politeness; and supper being ended, they talked of business". The summoning of spirits to feast on corpses here feels more like a middle-class dinner party than a diabolical act.

After a slight lull in the production of Gothic texts in the 1770s and 1780s, the 1790s marked a high point in 18th-century Gothic romance. The existence of circulating libraries and the production of books with cheap card covers made literature more accessible than ever, and the reading public wanted the Gothic. It's no coincidence that the rapid rise in the popularity of the genre in this decade occurred alongside the violent and bloody events of the French Revolution and the European wars which followed. As Fred Botting observes:

> Terror… had an overwhelming political significance in the period. The decade of the French Revolution saw the most violent of challenges to monarchical order. In Britain the Revolution and the political radicalism it inspired were represented as a tide of destruction threatening the complete dissolution of the social order. In Gothic images of violence and excessive passion, in villainous threats to proper domestic structures, there is a significant overlap in literary and political metaphors of fear and anxiety.

This sense of terror fed into the work of Ann Radcliffe, who produced several bestselling Gothic novels during the 1790s. Like Walpole, Radcliffe was interested in ideas of lineage and identity, but her Gothic was less excessive than that produced by Walpole and Beckford. Radcliffe became known for her use of the "explained supernatural", whereby supposedly ghostly phenomena are ultimately attributed to earthly sources. In her novels, she avoids the depiction of violence and refuses to show the reader any objects of terror explicitly (her heroines have a habit of seeing something dreadful and then fainting before they can explain what it was); instead, Radcliffe builds narrative suspense and uses the power of suggestion.

The Italian, or the Confession of the Black Penitents, which went on sale in 1797, was the last of Radcliffe's novels to be published during her lifetime. *The Italian* is often read as a response to a novel called *The Monk* which had been published the previous year by Matthew Lewis, who subsequently became known as "Monk" Lewis due to the popularity, and reputation, of his text. This novel was explicit in its use of sex and violence, gleefully transgressing boundaries in its depictions – which at times border on the pornographic – of sex, incest, murder, and pacts with the devil.

In her own tale of an evil monk, Radcliffe uses Catholic Italy to explore how ancient values – encapsulating superstition and corruption – threaten the modern. In writing the novel, she sought to reaffirm her own established aesthetics of terror, and in the process rejected Lewis's use of explicit horror. This distinction between terror and horror was explored by Radcliffe in an essay written in around 1802, but not published until 1826, entitled "On the Supernatural in Poetry". In this essay, she argued that terror and horror "are so far opposite, that the first expands the soul, and awakens the faculties to a high degree of life; the other contracts, freezes, and nearly annihilates them". For Radcliffe, terror was associated with the "uncertainty and obscurity" of the sublime. The sublime is an aesthetic concept suggesting everything that is boundless and cannot be understood, contained, or imitated. In his 1757 work *A Philosophical Enquiry into the Origin of Our Ideas of the Sublime and the Beautiful,* Edmund Burke had connected the sublime with that which is vast, great, dark, gloomy, solid, and massive.

In Radcliffe's Gothic novels, the sublime is linked with feeling and emotion, giving the reader an insight into the heroine's inner consciousness. In her extended, poetic descriptions of rugged and mountainous landscapes, Radcliffe sought to replicate the visual effects of contemporary paintings of such scenes, with the reader viewing these sublime scenes via the gaze of the protagonist.

Radcliffe's heroines often find themselves captured by evil villains, and when in *The Italian* Ellena finds herself imprisoned by the sinister Schedoni in the convent of San Stefano, she retreats to a turret to view a sublime landscape that prompts "dreadful pleasure" and "awaken[s] all her heart". By viewing this scene of cliffs, mountains, and forests, Ellena finds herself refreshed and strengthened, experiencing the very expansion of the soul and awakening of the faculties that Radcliffe argues is prompted by terror.

By the late 1790s, the Gothic had in many ways become rather formulaic, and it was this set of conventions (the persecuted heroine, the hidden passageway, the family secret) that Jane Austen parodied in *Northanger Abbey,* a send-up of the

Radcliffian Gothic that was published in 1818 but written c. 1798-99. When Mary Shelley started to write *Frankenstein, or The Modern Prometheus* in 1816, she reworked a set of established tropes into something that felt far more modern. By this point, the French Revolution was long over, and even the Napoleonic wars had come to an end. Rather than looking back to a medieval past or seeking to locate terror in anti-Catholic sentiment, Shelley chose to respond to recent discourses on radical politics, science, and sensibility. She was part of a group of writers known as the Romantics, who emphasised the importance of feeling and held the imagination, originality, and the spontaneous expression of the individual in high esteem.

Romanticism frequently looked to the individual's relationship with the natural world for inspiration, and many Romantic writers looked down on the popular Gothic mode of writing as inferior to the transcendental experience offered by nature. The poet William Wordsworth famously dismissed the popular "sickly and stupid German Tragedies" in his 1800 Preface to *Lyrical Ballads*, yet his own work – and that of other Romantics such as Percy Shelley and Lord Byron – was undoubtedly indebted to the 18th-century Gothic.

Victor Frankenstein, the protagonist of Mary Shelley's novel, is in many ways a Romantic: he is preoccupied with his individual art and seeks fulfilment by gaining power over nature. Like Vathek, Frankenstein has a thirst for knowledge, but he isn't seduced by magic and the supernatural; rather, he seeks to use science to play God and create the perfect man. Instead of a haunted castle or crumbling abbey, Frankenstein retreats to the laboratory, and in the place of a demon or spectre we are confronted with a flesh-and-blood monster. The creature may or may not be classed as "human" but it is very much alive and real, and in many ways its immediate violence and hideousness are more terrifying than a ghostly being that silently slides out of view.

In her Author's Introduction to a revised version of the novel published in 1831, Shelley explains that *Frankenstein* was written as part of a ghost-story writing competition suggested by her friend Lord Byron, and notes that she wanted to create a text that "would speak to the mysterious fears of our nature and awaken thrilling horror – one to make the reader dread to look round, to curdle the blood, and quicken the beatings of the heart". Shelley's text doesn't contain a ghost, but her idea – which came to her one night in a waking-dream – "haunted" her like a "hideous phantom".

In her depiction of the creature's monstrosity, Shelley explores the idea of difference and our treatment of those who are "other" – that is, not like us. The creature is not inherently evil, but rather comes to act in a violent and cruel way after having been rejected by society due to his hideous appearance. Both of Shelley's parents, who were writers themselves, had examined the idea of monstrosity within a political context. Her mother, Mary Wollstonecraft, had argued in *A Vindication of the Rights of Men* (1790) that "man has been changed into an artificial monster by the station in which he was born". Likewise, her father, William Godwin (to whom *Frankenstein* was dedicated), had suggested in his writings that monstrosity was a mark of cruel or corrupt socio-political structures, and argued that any monsters created by these systems reflect wider, more monstrous formations. In his *Enquiry Concerning Political Justice*, published in 1793, Godwin had described the feudal system as a "Voracious monster" whose legacy continued to give power and privilege to the aristocracy in the 18th century.

Inspired by her father's thinking, Shelley explored these ideas of monstrosity and justice in *Frankenstein*. When Justine – whose name, perhaps, suggests "justice" – is falsely accused of murder, Elizabeth, the orphan child who eventually marries Frankenstein, criticises the system that blamed and sentenced her, explaining that "men appear to me as monsters thirsting for each other's blood". In granting her Gothic monster a voice, Shelley seeks to deconstruct our understanding of monstrosity, and makes us question whether the creature's monstrous nature is in fact created by a monstrous society.

Fin de Siècle Gothic

From the 1760s until the beginning of the 19th century, the Gothic was commonly set in a distant time or place and featured ghosts, monsters and villains who appeared far removed from the everyday reality of the reader. During the early Victorian, period, however, the Gothic came to be more familiar, set in domestic scenes and intruding upon family life. In texts such as Emily Brontë's *Wuthering Heights* and Charlotte Brontë's *Jane Eyre* (both published in 1847), the threat of the Gothic is located in the intrusion of the "other" into stable, domestic settings: both Heathcliff and Bertha Mason are outsiders, with their dark, foreign appearances translating into monstrosity and violence. Likewise, in the "sensation" novel that became popular in the 1860s and 1870s, blackmail, deception, madness, and murder all threaten Christian moral values and social conformity.

The Gothic experienced a surge in popularity at the end of the 19th century: a period known as the *fin de siècle* (end of the century). Just as the Gothic texts of the 18th century and Romantic period were influenced by the politics and intellectual concerns of the age, so too was the Gothic of the 1880s and 1890s inspired by the interests and anxieties of the era. The *fin de siècle* marked a time of great uncertainty for the late Victorians: the Queen, who had come to the throne in 1837, was entering old age, and the celebrated century was drawing to a

Robert Louis Stevenson (1850 - 1894)

close. While the mid-century Victorians had considered themselves to be continually "improving" (scientifically, culturally, economically, and socially), by the 1880s there was a fear that this rate of progress couldn't continue and that society would inevitably begin to decline.

As the dawn of the 20th century loomed, nobody was quite sure what was going to happen next. Key to this anxiety was the concept of "degeneration": the idea that society was declining towards an inferior condition. One of the most prominent theorists on the threat of degeneration was Max Nordau, who in a work of 1895 called *Degeneration* referred to the current epoch as the "Dusk of Nations", arguing that the "day is over" and the shadowy night of the unknown coming era "draws on". Nordau links degeneration with the "decadence" of the *fin de siècle* period, which was associated with the lifestyle of the aristocracy and characterised by refinement, an interest in artifice, and moral decay.

This fear of degeneration is central to the Gothic literature produced in the period, which transformed the traditional Gothic motif of the ruined castle or crumbling abbey into an exploration of the decaying mind and body whereby the human becomes monstrous. The growth of cities provided the perfect setting for this new breed of Gothic, with their dark and labyrinthine streets replacing the hidden galleries and subterranean passageways of the first wave of Gothic novels. The city provided a sense of anonymity, and it was perfectly possible to assume a veneer of respectability while secretly disappearing into dark alleyways and criminal dens to partake in illicit behaviour. Combined with a growing interest in psychology and the workings of the mind (particularly the criminal mind), this resulted in the concept of the plurality of the self; a single person could now effectively lead multiple lives with different personalities.

In Oscar Wilde's *The Picture of Dorian Gray*, which was originally printed in 1890 in *Lippincott's Monthly Magazine* before being published in book form the following year, the implications of living a double life are drawn out to create a distinctly Gothic tale. Dorian Gray is a beautiful young man who is seduced by decadence and descends into a life of cruelty and lies. He is able to hide this behaviour, however, due to the fact that his own physical appearance does not reflect his immoral lifestyle; rather, a portrait painted by his friend Basil Hallward ages and decays instead – a "loathsome" double of Dorian that reveals the extent of his moral corruption.

This doubling is a common device in Gothic texts, and is a form of a phenomenon known as the "uncanny"; that is, a sense of unfamiliarity at the heart of the familiar that prompts feelings of strangeness or eeriness. The concept of the uncanny is generally acknowledged to have been developed by the father of psychoanalysis, Sigmund Freud, who, in an essay of 1919, argued that the German word *unheimlich* ("unhomely") suggests that which is both homely and hidden. As a form of the uncanny, the double – or *doppelgänger* – prompts anxiety due to its repetition. The repetition of experience, or *déjà vu*, suggests both doubling and deception within the familiar.

This idea was also used by Robert Louis Stevenson in *The Strange Case of Dr Jekyll and Mr Hyde* (1886), in which the respectable Dr Jekyll transforms into an evil, criminal double. Like Dorian's portrait, this double is ugly, with Hyde's troglodytic appearance suggesting his degeneration. The use of the uncanny double, however, is not exclusive to *fin de siècle* Gothic literature; Frankenstein's monster can be read as a double of his creator, with Frankenstein himself referring to the creature as "my own vampire, my own spirit let loose from the grave".

By hiding his portrait away from the world, Dorian turns his double into a kind of internal conscience. This reading is enhanced if we consider that Dorian stores the picture in the attic of his house, a space which becomes the head, or mind, if we "biologise" the building (as Gothic writers from Walpole onwards have often done). While his *doppelgänger* grows increasingly hideous, Dorian is able to steal away to the dark peripheries of the city, frequenting opium dens and eventually committing murder.

This *fin de siècle* fascination with degeneration, criminal behaviour, and the Gothic lurking in our everyday world is also found in Bram Stoker's *Dracula*, a vampire novel that was published in 1897.[*] If Dorian's crimes are largely hidden from sight – even for the reader – then Count Dracula's are presented in gory and explicit detail. Dracula, as a foreigner from Transylvania, can be read as a response to contemporary fears about immigration, particularly from Eastern Europe; long used to being the coloniser, by the end of the 19th century Britain was feeling threatened by reverse colonisation and the potential degeneration that this implied. In biting and sucking the life blood

---

[*] Stoker wasn't the first writer to imagine Gothic monstrosity in vampiric terms; John Polidori – another participant in Byron's ghost-story writing competition – had published a short tale called *The Vampyre* in 1819, with James Malcolm Rymer and Sheridan Le Fanu publishing Gothic vampire narratives in 1847 and 1872 respectively.

from his victims, Dracula invades and infects modern England, threatening to become "the father or furtherer of a new order of beings, whose road must lead through Death, not Life".

In other words, this foreign vampire is perceived as having the potential to transform civilised and moral British citizens into a new, degenerate race, taking over their bodies from the inside. Where Gothic novels of the 18th century had frequently used external sites, such as medieval castles, as locations for ghosts to occupy, Stoker transforms the human body itself into a space that is invaded and "haunted" by the supernatural. Dracula is a parasitic creature with an affinity for animals such as wolves and bats; his atavism and criminality are attributed to his "child-brain" and "imperfectly formed mind" – a sign of his degenerate nature.* In depicting his monstrous villain in this way, Stoker was drawing on the contemporary thinking of Cesare Lombroso, an Italian criminologist who is, in fact, referred to within the novel. Lombroso theorised that criminality is an inherited trait, with criminals displaying primitive, savage, or sub-human traits.

Both *The Picture of Dorian Gray* and *Dracula* explore *fin de siècle* anxieties within the context of transgressive sexual behaviour: in *Dorian Gray*, this transgression takes the form of suggestions about homosexuality (which was illegal at the time), while

---

* "Atavism" suggests that which is an evolutionary throwback, displaying ancestral traits that have reappeared.

Dracula explores the dangers of sexual promiscuity. Not only does Count Dracula spread his infection through blood (suggesting, perhaps, the transmission of a sexually transmitted disease), but his young, female, middle-class victims represent the exploitation of such women by decadent aristocrats. As a woman who at one point expresses sorrow that she cannot marry three men, Lucy is particularly vulnerable to the Count's infection, and her transformation into a vampire is unsurprisingly depicted in terms of a sexual fall.

Upon becoming a vampire, her purity is said to change into "voluptuous wantonness"; her sexuality is indicated by her "opened red lips", and her blood-stained white dress symbolises her loss of innocence in distinctly sexual terms. Her loss of virtuous, feminine qualities is made all the more apparent when she is observed murdering a child with cold-blooded cruelty, rejecting what should be natural maternal feelings in an act of violence and callousness. The sexualisation of Lucy's monstrosity is continued into her death, with Arthur's "untrembling arm" described as rising and falling as he drives the stake "deeper and deeper" into her heart in order to kill her, and therefore save her from her own unnatural impulses. As Lucy writhes and quivers beneath him, Arthur's face reveals his "high duty" to destroy this impure creature; once the act is complete, his face shines with a "glad, strange light" that betrays his relief at having defeated the transgressive threat of a violent and predatory female.

Like a number of Gothic novels written across the 18th and 19th centuries, *Dracula* comprises a number of distinct voices that are collected together to form the narrative. Where novels such as Charles Robert Maturin's *Melmoth the Wanderer* (1820), however, were structured around a series of stories-within-stories that spanned place and time, *Dracula* is an epistolary text, formed from a collection of contemporary journals, letters, and clippings. Rather than confusing the reader with its mix of voices like many of its predecessors, then, the novel is presented as rational and scientific, collecting together evidence about the nature of Dracula and the fate of his victims.

Indeed, the novel deliberately references a number of new technologies that mark the late Victorian period out as an advanced and civilised age, mentioning telephones and typewriters as well as alluding to modern thinkers like Nordau and Lombroso. It is this modern, rational version of England that Count Dracula – as a representative of a feudal, superstitious old Europe – threatens. Dracula, in his gruesome and bestial corporeality, is more real than the ghosts and phantoms of earlier Gothic novels, yet he is simultaneously difficult to define. This monster is part human and part beast, living among humans but also supernatural. As a member of the "undead", he even transgresses the boundary between life and death: a state that is very much at odds with the certainty and rationality of the modern world.

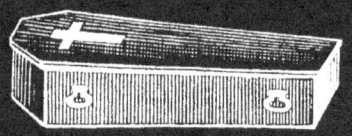

FIVE FACTS ABOUT THE GOTHIC

1. Like Horace Walpole before him, William Beckford pretended that Vathek was translated from a found manuscript. The Preface to the 1786 edition claims that the original story was "collected in the East by a Man of letters". This technique distances the reader from the text, making it seem more exotic and strange.

2. Although it was a huge commercial success when it was first published, *Dracula* was actually outsold at the time by another Gothic novel of 1897, Richard Marsh's *The Beetle*, which tells the story of a fantastical Egyptian creature seeking revenge in *fin de siècle* London.

3. Many people in the 18th century felt that Gothic literature was dangerous in the hands of impressionable female readers. One correspondent to the Monthly Magazine and British Register in 1797 described Gothic novels as "trash" and a "disgrace" to public libraries.

4. *Frankenstein* was not Mary Shelley's only Gothic work: she also explored monstrosity, immortality, and the 'double' in her short stories "The Mourner'"(1830), "Transformation" (1831), and "The Mortal Immortal" (1833).

5. Bram Stoker wrote a theatrical adaptation of *Dracula* called *Count Dracula: or The Un-Dead* in 1897. Stoker created the play in order to protect the dramatic rights to his book.

Portrait of Horace Walpole by Rosalba Carriera, circa 1741

Twentieth-century British Gothic

As the Gothic moved into the 20th century, it continued to respond to the contemporary intellectual and cultural climate. The ghost story became a popular genre, with Algernon Blackwood and M. R. James publishing collections of ghost stories in the first decades of the century, but the post-World War One period saw a preference for realism and a consequent lull in the creation of Gothic literature. With the rise of post-structuralism – a school of thought suggesting that meaning is inherently unstable – from the late 1960s onwards, the Gothic came to be re-examined and the potential of its plurality and excess embraced. As Angela Carter wrote in the Afterword to *Fireworks*, a collection of her short stories published in 1974: "We live in Gothic times."

Although the Gothic appears in several of Carter's works, it is perhaps most prominent in a collection of short tales published in 1979 entitled *The Bloody Chamber and Other Stories*. In this collection, Carter was able to use the excessive nature of the Gothic and the freedom from realism that it granted to break taboos and cross borders. These reworkings of traditional fairy stories are used by Carter to challenge conventional gender roles and show us alternatives to the patriarchy. In this sense, Carter's texts can be considered to be "postmodern"; that is, they question the constructions that we accept as truth and present marginalised figures – in this case, women – for our reconsideration.

Postmodern texts are sceptical about originality, and are self-aware in their consciousness of the traditions from which they originate. In choosing to rewrite fairy tales, Carter uses a form with which we are familiar from childhood as a means through which we learn life lessons, but simultaneously twists the "truth" of these texts to reveal a different perspective. This shift in perspective, however, is certainly not dependent on simple binary oppositions: "The Courtship of Mr Lyon" and "The Tiger's Bride" both respond to "Beauty and the Beast", offering alternative takes on the original tale.

The tales included in *The Bloody Chamber* aren't stand-alone: they function as a unit, using Gothic unease to make us consider what we take for granted before showing us alternatives. While the backdrop of these tales is comfortingly familiar for the reader, Carter's use of sexual imagery, crude language, and bloody violence is destabilising. Always keeping the precedent set by her predecessors in mind, she engages with Gothic writers such as Edgar Allan Poe in her depiction of a gruesome torture chamber in "The Bloody Chamber", combining a genre linked with innocence and instruction with tales of terror and gratuitous violence. Likewise, our expectations of women in these texts are consistently challenged when Carter – writing during the "second wave" of feminism – grants her heroines power and agency rather than depicting them as the passive, helpless victims familiar from fairy tales.

In "The Company of Wolves", a reworking of "Little Red Riding Hood", our heroine does not cower in fear when the wolf declares that his big teeth are "All the better to eat you with". Instead, the young girl bursts out laughing because "she knew she was nobody's meat", a statement that suggests bodily and sexual autonomy as well as an assuredness that she won't be eaten. In a reversal of our expectations, it is the female who takes control of the situation, ripping off the predator's shirt in an act of sexual assertiveness before discarding her own clothing. After the act of copulation, the wolf lays his "fearful" head upon her lap in a show of submissiveness and allows her to groom him before taking her in a "tender" embrace.

While the fantasy worlds of these tales at first seem fantastic and removed from our everyday lives, it soon becomes apparent that they have much to teach us about our understanding of our own society, particularly in terms of the assumptions that we make.

In her reworking of fairy tales, Carter also responds to the female Gothic of authors such as Radcliffe, reworking the traditional persecuted heroine trope in her depictions of strong, autonomous women who overcome Gothic villains without the help of (male) heroes. "The Bloody

Chamber" uses the traditional space of the Gothic castle in a familiar way, presenting it as holding fearful secrets within its hidden spaces and setting it in isolation from the rest of the world. Like any number of Radcliffe's heroines, Carter's nameless narrator is trapped in the castle, and forbidden to enter the "private study" of her new husband which, it transpires, is a torture chamber.

Ellen Moers, the first critic to use the term "Female Gothic", suggests that such situations represent a fear of domestic entrapment for women, and this would certainly seem to be the case for Carter's young newlywed. Rather than being rescued by a hero, however, Carter's heroine is liberated by her own mother, who appears like a "wild thing" on a horse to kill her daughter's husband. In Radcliffe's work, mothers are frequently absent, and when Ellena's mother returns in *The Italian*, it is to reveal her daughter's true lineage and facilitate her marriage. For Carter, in contrast, the maternal figure returns at the end of the text to break down the institution of marriage and save her daughter.

This postmodern re-examination of roles and identity, including the artificial "performance" of gender, is also found at work in *The Wasp Factory*, a Gothic novel of 1984 by the Scottish author Iain Banks. Just as contemporary reviewers of early Gothic novels such as *The Monk* were horrified by the violence and excess of the genre, so too did initial reviews of *The Wasp Factory* express unease and even disgust: *Punch* called the novel "a bad dream of a book", while a writer for the *Mail on Sunday* declared: "If a nastier, more vicious or distasteful novel appears this spring, I shall be surprised." The narrative is told from the perspective of Frank, a psychopathic teenager who believes that she is a castrated boy but, it transpires, is actually a girl. This deception is made possible by Frank's father, a scientist who mocks up the supposed remains of his child's genitals and uses hormone tablets to fool Frances into thinking that she is Francis.

The instability of identity is a common concern in the Gothic novel, provoking feelings of unease, suspicion, or discombobulation in the reader. In *The Italian*, it transpires that Ellena's parentage is not as initially thought, while Frankenstein's monster despairs that he was "created apparently united by no link to any other being in existence", explaining that he initially repeatedly asked himself: "Who was I? What was I?" Even though the clash between Frank's biological sex and the gender that she has been living as isn't revealed until the end of the text, uncertainties concerning her identity are raised from the opening chapter of the novel. Frank reveals that her birth was never registered, meaning that she has no birth certificate, no National Insurance number, and "nothing to say I'm alive or have ever existed".

She ultimately comes to theorise that she behaved in the way she did (murdering three children and committing other acts of torture and violence) because of her sexual identity, speculating that she chose to destroy because she had been led to believe that she couldn't procreate. When Frank argues that her child victims were, at the point of their deaths, "no more able to perform the required act than I was", she explicitly refers to sexual performance while implicitly analysing her gender performance, proceeding to remark: "Talk about penis envy."

Like *The Bloody Chamber*, *The Wasp Factory* is both depraved and darkly comic. Amongst examinations of murder and ritualistic torture, we find moments of humour such as Frank experiencing an attack from a giant rabbit. This episode transforms a small, furry creature into a truly Gothic monster with "lips curled back, teeth long and yellow" – a description that would not be out of place in a vampire novel such as *Dracula*.

The Gothic novel of the past that would appear to have influenced Banks the most, though, is *Frankenstein*; indeed, *The Wasp Factory* is in many ways a postmodern rewriting of this Romantic text. Frank's father functions as a kind of Frankenstein figure (the echo between the names here is no coincidence), conducting experiments in a locked study that Frank speculates contains "a secret". This secret, of course, transpires to be concerned with the monstrosity of an engineered body; just as Frankenstein constructs his monster from dismembered corpses, so Frank's father constructs the fantasy of a mutilated, monstrous body for his daughter.

Southern Gothic

The Gothic became popular in the United States in the early 19th century, at a time when the prevalent ideal of America as a self-made and free society was haunted by deep-rooted anxieties concerning class and race. While the Emancipation Proclamation of 1863 (followed by the Thirteenth Amendment of 1865) ended the legal institution of slavery in the States, the legacy of slavery led to the continuation of racial tensions, particularly in the South. In the 20th century the so-called Jim Crow laws, which enforced racial segregation and led to numerous social and economic disadvantages for African Americans living in the Southern United States, continued until 1965. As a response to both these racial tensions and a sense of the South as impoverished and isolated from the rest of the United States, a new breed of Gothic known as the "Southern Gothic" emerged.

In works of Southern Gothic literature, both black and white writers have used the grotesque and the uncanny to examine how deeply-embedded racial tensions and inequalities continued to trouble the South throughout the 19th and 20th centuries. Southern Gothic texts are often marked by horror, violence, and a sense of decay; while the United

States does not have a medieval past filled with castles, abbeys, and catacombs upon which to draw in its presentation of the Gothic, its history nonetheless succeeds in haunting its present.

William Faulkner, author of *Sanctuary* (1931) and *Absalom, Absalom!* (1936), is one of the defining figures of Southern Gothic literature written in the first half of the 20th century. *Light in August*, a modernist text published in 1932, relates the story of Joe Christmas, a man from the Deep South who looks white but is rumoured to be mixed race. Like other writers of the Gothic, Faulkner explores the idea of the fractured self in this text, exploring how Joe's uncertain identity leads to him being "othered" by those around him. As a result of his ambiguous racial ancestry, he is unable to find acceptance in the white communities of a segregated South, but nor is he able to integrate fully amongst black people.

Living "as man and wife" with a woman who is said to resemble an "ebony carving", he makes a conscious effort to become black; lying awake beside the woman in the dead of night, he attempts to breathe in "the dark and inscrutable thinking and being of negroes" while breathing out "the white blood and the white thinking and being". Despite appearing white, Joe is feared by those of certain white heritage, and finds himself accused when a white woman is found brutally murdered.

Faulkner was not the first writer of Gothic fiction to explore how the perception of monstrosity can be influenced by such racial "othering"; in Emily

Brontë's *Wuthering Heights*, for example, the "dirty, ragged, black-haired" orphan Heathcliff is described by his white adoptive family as a "gipsy brat" and is said to be "as dark almost as if it came from the devil". Likewise, some critics have argued that Mary Shelley's depiction of the monster in *Frankenstein* – a book written in the wake of the Slave Trade Act of 1807 that abolished the slave trade in the British Empire – drew upon contemporary descriptions of black people.

Light in August deals explicitly with the legacy of the end of slavery in the American South, with the burning house alluded to in the novel's title belonging to a woman whose family, the Burdens, were hated white abolitionists. There is no suggestion of the supernatural in the text, but this house could nevertheless be said to be "haunted" in the sense that it is occupied by the ghosts of the past. The structure of the narrative reinforces the idea that the past continues to haunt the present, with flashbacks disorientating the reader and revealing the story piece by piece.

Running in parallel with Joe's tale is that of Lena Grove, a young pregnant woman who is similarly ostracised due to her status as an unmarried mother. Like Joe Christmas, she is a wanderer, travelling from Alabama to Mississippi in search of her child's father, Lucas Burch, who reinvents himself as Joe Brown in an attempt to elude his former lover. Several characters in the text either change their name or are mistaken for others due to the similarity

Toni Morrison, author of Beloved

of their names: just as he is unsure of his racial heritage, Joe Christmas does not know his "real" name due to being abandoned as a child; he is then renamed Joe McEachern when he is adopted by a devout Christian couple who see his original name as "heathenish"; Lena comes across a man named Byron Bunch when looking for Lucas Burch; and Lucas Burch, as Joe Brown, comes to partner up with fellow outcast, and fellow Joe, Joe Christmas.

Like the narrative flashbacks and shifts between the concurrent stories of Lena and Joe Christmas, these shifting, fragmented, and unstable identities serve to confuse us, leaving us feeling as alienated and unsure as the characters in the text. Even the text itself can be seen to split into different layers due to the fact that it can be read as allegory (that is, a story with a double meaning that can be interpreted on two levels). The wandering Lena and her child can be read as a representation of the Virgin Mary and Christ, while Byron Bunch functions as the Joseph figure that Joe Brown refuses to be.

Biblical themes can also be found in a later work of Southern Gothic: Cormac McCarthy's *Outer Dark* (1968). Like *Light in August*, this novel comprises two narrative threads, telling the stories of Rinthy and Culla Holmes, two siblings from somewhere in Appalachia. The brother and sister have an incestuous relationship that results in the birth of a child; Culla leaves the baby to die of exposure, telling Rinthy that it died of natural causes, but it is found by a tinker who takes it away. While Rinthy sets off in pursuit of the tinker in order to retrieve her child (much like Lena seeking Lucas Burch), Culla wanders in parallel, drifting aimlessly and arousing suspicion in every community that he enters.

The title *Outer Dark* is taken from the Gospel of Matthew, in which hell is described as a place of "outer darkness" filled with torment and the "weeping and gnashing of teeth". The novel is in many ways hellish, and opens with Culla having a dream in which the sun turns dark and the world becomes cold. The vision echoes the description of the apocalypse – that is, the end of the world – depicted in both Matthew and Revelation, the final book of the Bible. This sense of hell and apocalypse continues throughout the text, with the landscape of the American South marred by a feeling of decay and horror.

As Culla wanders on his journey, he is stalked by three men who carry out terrible acts of violence and depravity. It is uncertain whether these shadowy figures are real, separate entities or a projection of Culla's evil – often, they are presented as both simultaneously. When they encounter the tinker, for example, it is said that they "*might have risen from the ground*" like phantoms; the trio immediately become more earthly and corporeal, however, when one of them smiles at the tinker while holding a rifle. Likewise, when Culla encounters them for the second time, they are described as "revenants" wearing the same clothes and adopting the same attitudes as before, but although they are "spectral" they are also "palpable as stone".

Here, McCarthy is experimenting with the idea of the ghostly. As readers of the Gothic, we are familiar with being scared by spectres while simultaneously maintaining an awareness that they cannot do any real bodily harm. McCarthy's trio, however, are as shadowy and terrifying as ghosts, yet are still able to commit very real – and very extreme – acts of violence, including murder and cannibalism. The threat of that which haunts is thus transformed in the novel into full-blown horror, shocking the reader and reconfiguring our expectations of this Gothic motif.

The conflation of that which seems supernatural with that which is marked by physical harm or violence occurs at several points in the text. When Culla is accused of prompting a herd of swine to stampede, the reader is reminded of Matthew 8 (28-32), in which Christ casts a group of devils out of two men and into some nearby pigs, which promptly run off a cliff to their deaths. While the event in the novel itself isn't supernatural, this link with demonic possession is unsettling for the reader, and makes us wonder why ill fortune and chaos strike wherever Culla goes.

Similarly, Culla's crossing of the river with the ferryman is reminiscent of Greek mythology, in which the river Styx must be crossed in order to enter Hades, the underworld. Culla certainly finds himself in a hellish place when he reaches the opposite bank of the river, encountering the trio of evil men and becoming increasingly uneasy in their presence. In many ways, the text can be read as a parable in its presentation of the journeys of Culla and Rinthy; while Rinthy is presented as good, innocent, and maternal, Culla is unable to escape his sin. The text ends when Culla reaches the end of the road and finds a stale, stagnant swamp described as a "spectral waste" rearing nothing but "naked trees in attitudes of agony". This apocalyptic space suggests ruin and infertility, representative not only of Culla's past but also suggesting that there is no hope for his future.

The blurring of the natural and the supernatural is an important concern in *Beloved*, a novel by Toni Morrison that was published in 1987 and won the

Pulitzer Prize for Fiction in 1988. A work of African American Gothic, the novel is set in Kentucky and Ohio in the mid – to late-19th century and explores the aftermath of slavery for the South. Like *Light in August*, it explores how the transgressions of the past have the potential to haunt the present, but unlike its predecessor the story is told by a black author from the point of view of the African Americans who were enslaved.

In her Foreword to the novel, Morrison explains that she wrote *Beloved* after leaving her job, and was prompted by the "shock of liberation" to think about "what 'free' could possibly mean to women":

> In the eighties, the debate was still rolling: equal pay, equal treatment, access to professions, schools... and choice without stigma. To marry or not. To have children or not. Inevitably these thoughts led me to the different history of black women in this country – a history in which marriage was discouraged, impossible, or illegal; in which birthing children was required, but "having" them, being responsible for them – being, in other words, their parent – was as out of the question as freedom.

Beloved tells the story of a woman who felt she had no choice but to kill her child – who was buried as "Beloved" – rather than return her to a life of slavery. Inspired by the historical story of Margaret Garner, a young mother who escaped slavery and was arrested for murdering one child and attempting to murder the others rather than returning them to the plantation, Morrison argues that she uses her novel to relate African American women's history to "contemporary issues about freedom, responsibility, and women's 'place'". In other words, like so many other writers of the Gothic before her, Morrison uses the Gothic – which may in many ways seem utterly removed from reality – to explore the concerns and anxieties of her contemporary society, even as she sets her text in the past.

Initially, it seems that *Beloved* is going to be a conventional Gothic "haunted house" story. The novel opens with the revelation that a household has been broken apart by a haunting, with two boys running away from home due to ghostly activity (including the shattering of a mirror and the appearance of two tiny hand prints in a cake). However, it becomes unclear whether Beloved is a genuine spectre or merely a psychological projection of her mother's guilt. At times she seems grotesquely corporeal and real – her pregnant body growing bigger as she comes to dominate the household – but at other times her haunting is perceived as distinctly supernatural, with members of the community hearing the voices of "the black and angry dead" coming from inside the family home. Likewise, Beloved's death can be read in different ways. In some respects, it resembles the exorcism of a supernatural spirit, with a group of local women coming together and singing outside the house, their voices breaking over Sethe, who finds herself "baptized" in the wash. Faced with this confrontation, Beloved – described as the "devil-child" – disappears, with some claiming that she "exploded right before their eyes". Others simply think that she goes to hide out in the trees. Whatever the manner of Beloved's death, however, she is ultimately banished, and her haunting – whether supernatural or psychological – comes to an end.

As in both *Light in August* and *Outer Dark*, then, Morrison's tale of the Southern Gothic examines how the "ghosts" of the past – memories, legacies, and histories – continue to invade the present. Like Faulkner, Morrison uses flashbacks to disrupt the linear flow of the narrative, which emphasises this haunting process whereby the events of long ago continue to seep into and shape present-day life. Just as Mary Shelley before her constructed *Frankenstein* around a series of narrative voices enclosed around each other like a series of Chinese boxes, so Morrison uses different voices in her text to show different perspectives and to make us question the assumption that there is one single version of the truth or one sole source of authority. While Shelley's narrative structure has a suffocating effect due to the fact that each tale is "buried" within another, all of the voices in her text do at least remain distinct and identifiable. In contrast, Morrison's narrative voices sometimes overlap, leading to confusion and disorientation for the reader.

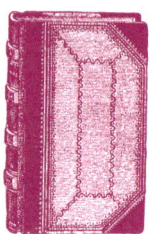

THE GOTHIC: A SHORT CHRONOLOGY

1764 Horace Walpole, *The Castle of Otranto* (the first Gothic novel)

1777 Clara Reeve, *The Champion of Virtue* (reissued the following year as *The Old English Baron*)

1786 William Beckford, *Vathek*

1790 Ann Radcliffe, *A Sicilian Romance*

1791 Ann Radcliffe, *The Romance of the Forest*

1794 Ann Radcliffe, *The Mysteries of Udolpho*

1796 Matthew Lewis, *The Monk*

1797 Ann Radcliffe, *The Italian*

1806 Charlotte Dacre, *Zofloya, or The Moor*

1818 Jane Austen, *Northanger Abbey*

1818 Mary Shelley, *Frankenstein*

1820 Charles Robert Maturin, *Melmoth the Wanderer*

1839 Edgar Allan Poe, "The Fall of the House of Usher"

1847 Charlotte Brontë, *Jane Eyre*

1847 Emily Brontë, *Wuthering Heights*

1860 Wilkie Collins, *The Woman in White*

1886 Robert Louis Stevenson, *The Strange Case of Dr Jekyll and Mr Hyde*

1890 Oscar Wilde, *The Picture of Dorian Gray* (reissued in expanded book form in 1891)

1897 Bram Stoker, *Dracula*
    Richard Marsh, *The Beetle*

1932 William Faulkner, *Light in August*

1938 Daphne du Maurier, *Rebecca*

1959 Shirley Jackson, *The Haunting of Hill House*

1968 Cormac McCarthy, *Outer Dark*

1979 Angela Carter, *The Bloody Chamber*

1983 Susan Hill, *The Woman in Black*

1984 Iain Banks, *The Wasp Factory*

1987 Toni Morrison, *Beloved*

FURTHER READING

Primary texts

Banks, Iain, *The Wasp Factory* (London: Abacus, 2013)

Beckford, William, *Vathek*, ed. by Thomas Keymer (Oxford: Oxford University Press, 2013)

Carter, Angela, *The Bloody Chamber and Other Stories* (London: Vintage, 2014)

Faulkner, William, *Light in August* (London: Vintage, 2005)

McCarthy, Cormac, *Outer Dark* (London: Picador, 2010)

Morrison, Toni, *Beloved* (London: Vintage, 2007)

Radcliffe, Ann, *The Italian*, ed. by Frederick Garber (Oxford: Oxford University Press, 2008)

Shelley, Mary, *Frankenstein, or, The Modern Prometheus: The 1818 Text,* ed. by Marilyn Butler (Oxford: Oxford University Press, 2008)

Stoker, Bram, *Dracula*, ed. by Roger Luckhurst (Oxford: Oxford University Press, 2011)

Wilde, Oscar, *The Picture of Dorian Gray*, ed. by Joseph Bristow (Oxford: Oxford University Press, 2008)

Secondary texts

Botting, Fred, *Gothic*, 2nd edn (London: Routledge, 2014)

Halberstam, Judith, *Skin Shows: Gothic Horror and the Technology of Monsters* (Durham: Duke University Press, 1995)

Hogle, Jerrold E., ed., *The Cambridge Companion to Gothic Fiction* (Cambridge: Cambridge University Press, 2002)
------, ed., *The Cambridge Companion to the Modern Gothic* (Cambridge: Cambridge University Press, 2014)

Moers, Ellen, *Literary Women* (London: W. H. Allen, 1977)

Punter, David, *The Literature of Terror: A History of Gothic Fictions from 1765 to the Present Day*, 2nd edn, 2 vols (London: Longman, 1996)
------, ed., *A New Companion to the Gothic*, 2nd edn (Chichester: Wiley-Blackwell, 2012)

Smith, Andrew, *Gothic Literature* (Edinburgh: Edinburgh University Press, 2007)

Spooner, Catherine, and Emma McEvoy, eds, *The Routledge Companion to the Gothic* (London: Routledge, 2007)

Wright, Angela, *Gothic Fiction* (Basingstoke: Palgrave Macmillan, 2007)

CG CONNELL GUIDES

Concise, intelligent guides to history and literature

CONNELL GUIDES TO LITERATURE

Novels and poetry
Emma
Far From the Madding Crowd
Frankenstein
Great Expectations
Hard Times
Heart of Darkness
Jane Eyre
Lord of the Flies
Mansfield Park
Middlemarch
Mrs Dalloway
Paradise Lost
Persuasion
Pride and Prejudice
Tess of the D'Urbervilles
The Canterbury Tales
The Great Gatsby
The Poetry of Robert Browning
The Waste Land
To Kill A Mockingbird
Wuthering Heights

Shakespeare
A Midsummer Night's Dream
Antony and Cleopatra
Hamlet
Julius Caesar
King Lear
Macbeth
Othello
Romeo and Juliet
The Second Tetralogy
The Tempest
Twelfth Night

Modern texts
A Doll's House
A Room with a View
A Streetcar Named Desire
An Inspector Calls
Animal Farm
Atonement
Beloved
Birdsong
Hullabaloo
Never Let Me Go
Of Mice and Men
Rebecca
Spies
The Bloody Chamber
The Catcher in the Rye
The History Boys
The Road
Vernon God Little
Waiting for Godot

NEW
A Short History of English Literature
American literature
Dystopian literature
How to write well
How to read Shakespeare
How to read a poem
How to write an essay
The Gothic
The poetry of Christina Rossetti
Women in literature

NEW: CONNELL GUIDES TO HISTORY

Guides
The French Revolution
Winston Churchill
World War One
The Rise and Fall of the Third Reich
The American Civil War
Stalin
Lenin
Nelson
The Tudors
Napoleon
The Cold War
The American Civil Rights Movement
The Normans
Russia and its Rulers

Short Guides
Britain after World War Two
Edward VI
Mary I
The General Strike
The Suffragettes

"Connell Guides should be required reading in every school in the country."
Julian Fellowes, creator of Downton Abbey

"What Connell Guides do is bring immediacy and clarity: brevity with depth. They unlock the complex and offer students an entry route."
Colin Hall, Head of Holland Park School

"These guides are a godsend. I'm so glad I found them."
Jessica Enthoven, A Level student, St Mary's Calne

To buy any of these guides, or for more information, go to
www.connellguides.com
Or contact us on (020)79932644 / info@connellguides.com

First published in 2017 by
Connell Guides
Spye Arch House
Spye Park
Lacock
Wiltshire
SN15 2PR

10 9 8 7 6 5 4 3 2 1

Copyright © Connell Guides Publishing Ltd.
All rights reserved. No part of this publication
may be reproduced, stored in a retrieval system or transmitted in any
form, or by any means (electronic, mechanical, or otherwise) without
the prior written permission of both the copyright owners
and the publisher.

A CIP catalogue record for this book is available from the British Library.
978-1-911187-60-8

Design © Nathan Burton
Assistant Editors:
Brian Scrivener and Paul Woodward

Printed in Great Britain

www.connellguides.com